D1412059

THE WORLD'S BIGGEST
AMPHIBIANS

by Mari Schuh

pogo

Ideas for Parents and Teachers

Pogo Books let children practice reading informational text while introducing them to nonfiction features such as headings, labels, sidebars, maps, and diagrams, as well as a table of contents, glossary, and index.

Carefully leveled text with a strong photo match offers early fluent readers the support they need to succeed.

Before Reading

- "Walk" through the book and point out the various nonfiction features. Ask the student what purpose each feature serves.
- Look at the glossary together. Read and discuss the words.

Read the Book

- Have the child read the book independently.
- Invite him or her to list questions that arise from reading.

After Reading

- Discuss the child's questions. Talk about how he or she might find answers to those questions.
- Prompt the child to think more. Ask: Have you ever caught a frog or a salamander? Was it heavy? How did its skin feel?

Pogo Books are published by Jump!
5357 Penn Avenue South
Minneapolis, MN 55419
www.jumplibrary.com

Library of Congress Cataloging-in-Publication Data

Schuh, Mari C., 1975- author.
  The world's biggest amphibians / by Mari Schuh.
    pages cm. – (The world's biggest animals)
  "Pogo Books are published by Jump!."
  Audience: Ages 7-10
  Includes index.
  ISBN 978-1-62031-209-4 (hardcover: alk. paper) –
  ISBN 978-1-62031-259-9 (paperback) –
  ISBN 978-1-62496-296-7 (ebook)
  1. Amphibians–Size–Juvenile literature.
  2. Amphibians–Juvenile literature. I. Title.
QL644.2.S3375 2016
597.8–dc23
                                        2015000273

Series Editor: Jenny Fretland VanVoorst
Series Designer: Anna Peterson
Photo Researcher: Anna Peterson

Photo Credits: Alamy, 14, 23; Animals Animals, cover; ardea, 15; Biosphoto, 7; Corbis, 3; National Geographic Creative, 1, 8-9; Nature Picture Library, 12-13, 18-19; Photoshot, 10-11; Science Source Images, 6; Shutterstock, 4; SuperStock, 16-17; Ted Papenfuss/CalPhotos, 20-21; Thinkstock, 5.

Printed in the United States of America at Corporate Graphics in North Mankato, Minnesota.

TABLE OF CONTENTS

CHAPTER 1

WHAT ARE AMPHIBIANS?

A toad sits in the warm sun.

A **salamander** lays eggs in a pond.

What do these animals have in common?

They are both **amphibians**. Amphibians live part of their lives in water and part on land.

They are **cold-blooded**. Their body temperature changes with their surroundings.

CHAPTER 2

HUGE FROGS

Frogs are a type of amphibian.

Goliath frogs are the biggest frogs in the world.

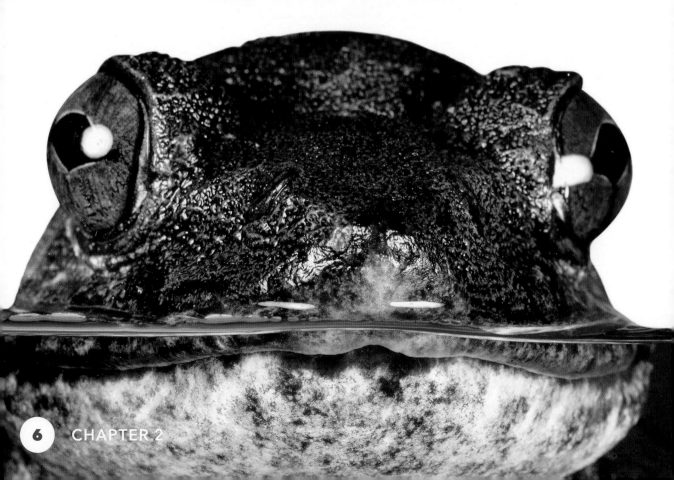

Goliath frogs can weigh seven pounds (3 kilograms).

That is more than two guinea pigs!

Goliath frogs have big bodies. Their body can be 12 inches (30 centimeters) long.

That is as long as a ruler!

Goliath frogs have long back legs. With their legs stretched out, goliath frogs can be almost 30 inches (76 cm) long.

That's as long as a skateboard!

DID YOU KNOW?

Goliath frogs can jump up to 10 feet (3 meters).

That is about the length of a small room!

body
12 in (30 cm)

stretched
30 in (76 cm)

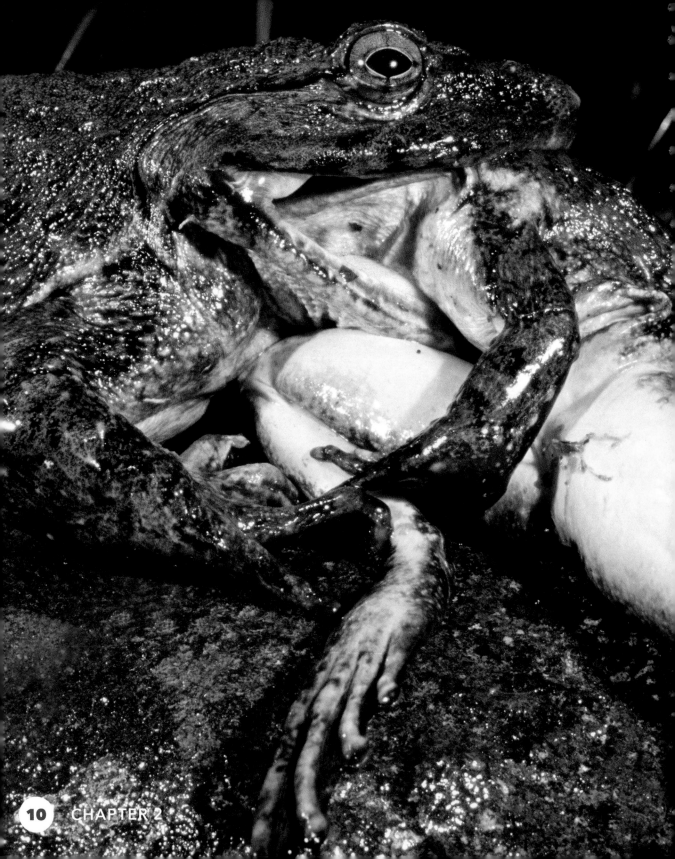

Goliath frogs look for food near rivers. They search at night.

Goliath frogs eat insects, fish, and small animals.

They also eat other frogs.

DID YOU KNOW?

Goliath frogs live near fast rivers. They have to be strong swimmers. Their slippery skin helps them move through the water. Their heavy body keeps them from being swept away.

WHERE ARE THEY?

Goliath frogs live in West Africa. These big frogs live in **rain forests**. They are found near waterfalls and fast rivers.

AFRICA

■ = Goliath Frog Range

Goliath frogs are the biggest frogs, but they aren't the biggest amphibians.

It takes 14 goliath frogs to match the weight of just one Chinese giant salamander.

CHAPTER 3

. . . .

SUPERSIZED SALAMANDERS

Chinese giant salamanders are the world's biggest amphibians.

They can weigh up to 100 pounds (45 kg).

That's more than a 10-year-old child!

Chinese giant salamanders are big and long.

They can be nearly six feet (1.8 meters) long.

That's bigger than many human adults!

DID YOU KNOW?

A Chinese giant salamander's tail can make up more than half its body length.

Chinese giant salamander

average human

prey

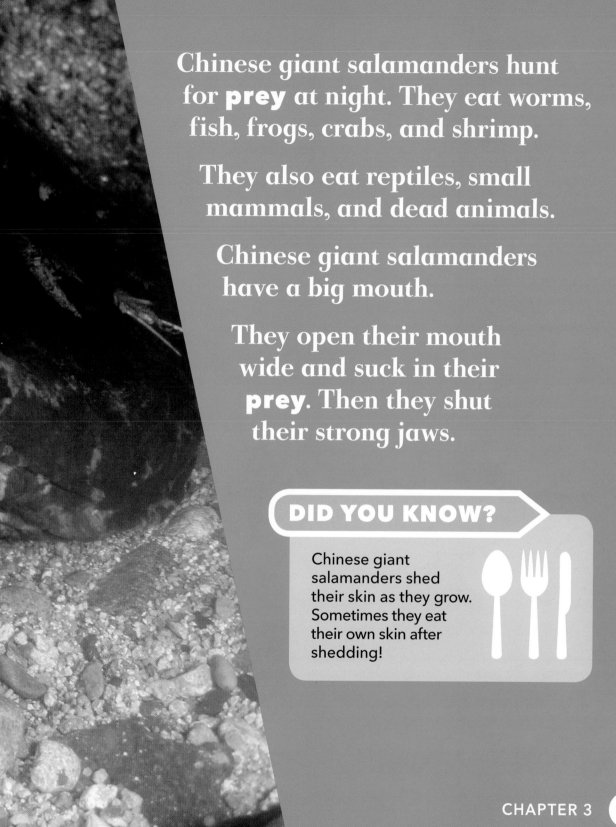

Chinese giant salamanders hunt for **prey** at night. They eat worms, fish, frogs, crabs, and shrimp.

They also eat reptiles, small mammals, and dead animals.

Chinese giant salamanders have a big mouth.

They open their mouth wide and suck in their **prey**. Then they shut their strong jaws.

DID YOU KNOW?

Chinese giant salamanders shed their skin as they grow. Sometimes they eat their own skin after shedding!

WHERE ARE THEY?

Chinese giant salamanders live in China. They live in areas with mountains and forests. They swim in **streams**, rivers, and lakes.

ASIA

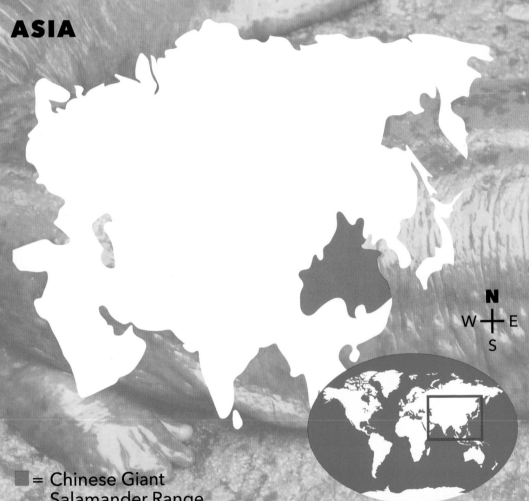

N
W ✛ E
S

= Chinese Giant
Salamander Range

Huge Chinese giant salamanders swim in rivers and lakes.

Big goliath frogs leap through the air.

What is the biggest amphibian you have ever seen?

ACTIVITIES & TOOLS

HOW HEAVY?

One Chinese giant salamander weighs as much as 14 goliath frogs. One goliath frog weighs as much as 140 common frogs.

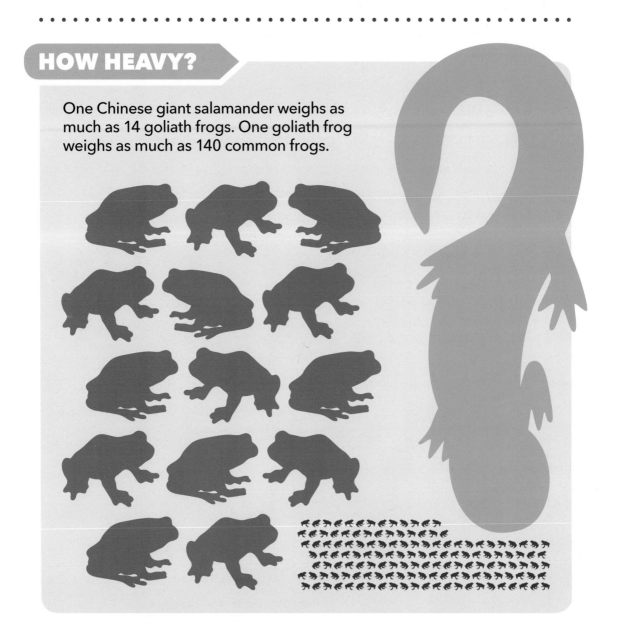

1. **Find an open area outside.**
2. **Jump like a frog! Take one big leap forward.**
3. **Have an adult measure your leap.**
4. **Jump again.**

Did you jump farther the second time? How does it compare to the length of a goliath frog's jump?

. . . .

GLOSSARY

amphibian: A cold-blooded animal that spends part of its life in water and part on land.

cold-blooded: Having a body temperature that changes with the surroundings.

frogs: A group of tailless leaping amphibians that have slender bodies, smooth, moist skin, and strong, long hind legs with webbed feet; frogs spend much of their time in the water.

prey: Insects and animals that are hunted for food.

rain forest: A thick area of trees where a lot of rain falls.

salamander: A group of amphibians that look like lizards but are covered with smooth, moist, scaleless skin.

stream: A small body of flowing water.

INDEX

TO LEARN MORE

Learning more is as easy as 1, 2, 3.

1) Go to www.factsurfer.com

2) Enter "biggestamphibians" into the search box.

3) Click the "Surf" to see a list of websites.

With factsurfer, finding more information is just a click away.